The *Gospel* Really Is *Good News*

JERRY ROBINSON

Copyright © 2021 Jerry Robinson
All rights reserved
First Edition

PAGE PUBLISHING, INC.
Conneaut Lake, PA

First originally published by Page Publishing 2021

ISBN 978-1-6624-3211-8 (pbk)
ISBN 978-1-6624-3212-5 (digital)

Printed in the United States of America

To my dear mother, the late Dorothy Robinson Carmack, from my youth, you showed me and my siblings Christ Jesus on a daily basis. You instilled into us the true meaning of unconditional love by demonstrating the life of Christ through your life. I thought of you often while writing this book.

Contents

Preface 7
Introduction 11
Chapter 1: Religion-ship 15
Chapter 2: Relationship 19
Chapter 3: Freedom 22
Chapter 4: The Cross 26
Chapter 5: How Can We Escape? 43
Chapter 6: The Birth of a New Baby 47
Chapter 7: We Are of What World? 56
Chapter 8: Seek Those Things Which Are Above 63
Chapter 9: The Order of Man 67
Chapter 10: Greater Is He That Is in You 71
Chapter 11: Who Is His Son? 77
Conclusion 81
Acknowledgments 85
Endorsements 87

Preface

"God Is My Co-Pilot." These are the words I read years ago on a car tag as I was walking across the parking lot toward the supermarket. My first thoughts were: *So that's our problem*! Instead of having God in the pilot seat where he belongs, he is in the co-pilot seat only to be called upon in a time of crisis or when we can't do all the right things ourselves. Ironically about a week later, I was at the same supermarket when I saw another car with a tag that read: "If you think you're perfect try walking on water" (this comes from Jesus walking on the water in John 6:19). Again the first thought that came to mind was, *Is walking on water the prerequisite for perfection?* Evidently, most think so. I wondered if that's why many reject Christ today because they can't live up to His expectations.

I wasn't raised in church at all. I can vaguely remember as a young child going to church on Easter morning. The reason that memory is so vivid is because I remember the egg hunt we had that morning after the service where I found the prize egg and was awarded five dollars! Today, five dollars isn't much, but in 1965 it was huge! It wasn't until after I married that I received Christ into my life and began going to church.

Like all new Christians, I was very ignorant when it came to the Bible. I could read it, but I definitely didn't understand it. An older Christian told me to start reading in First, Second and Third John, for they are the easiest to understand. But after reading these books, they were still Greek to me (no pun intended). I attended and eventually joined a Baptist church where it was drummed into me how to be born again (*at this particular church that's all they taught*). A few years later, I ventured into a Pentecostal church where I learned of the fullness of the Spirit. Yet the message for the most part was still the same. The focus was always on how to be born again but what we MUST do to stay born again.

Now let's fast-forward to the day when and why I was prompted to write this book. Many years have passed since my first experience with church as a youngster and my born again experience as a young adult. From there, I begin to teach Sunday school, then a few years later, I moved into the pastoral part of the ministry, where I've spent some twenty years (*I've since retired from pastoral ministry*). Let me briefly summarize how this book came about. I was about ten years into my ministry of preaching and teaching a relationship with Christ was by rules and regulations when I received the revelation of perfection.

I was reading Matthew 5:48 (KJV), where Jesus himself said these words, "Be ye therefore perfect even as your Father which is in heaven is perfect." I sensed something prompting me to read it again (later, I realized it was the Holy Spirit), so I read it again. It was like I was told to read it over and over so I read it over and over until I realized that this scripture did not say "Do ye therefore perfect it says BE ye therefore perfect." The Lord was telling me and is telling all of us his children to STOP trying to DO perfect when in reality, He is calling us to just BE perfect! Go ahead and BE what He has called you to be. Our Heavenly Father is calling us to live from perfection, not live for perfection!

A fresh new journey begins in our life when we fully understand what Jesus Christ has completely completed. The apostle Paul came into the knowledge of this completeness and penned these words: "And ye are complete in him, which is the head of all principality and power" (Colossians 2:10 KJV). Throughout this book, we will be sharing simple yet profound truths that have been hidden due to sincere but erroneous teaching.

I invite you to partake in the journey of fulfillment where we are no longer bound by religious expectations of man nor the church that can often offset the true Gospel of Christ. No longer should Old Testament law, which often accompanies the Gospel of grace the way grace is ineptly preached today in many churches (saved by grace, but live by law), bind us. We shall no longer be subjected to a so-called biblical legalism in any form which, may cause a man to look to his religious performance rather than Jesus's righteous performance—for our security is in Christ alone. Impatience for freedom shall be no more—for we are free!

Through the pages of this book, the intent is to unveil the mystery of the abundant life that resides inside of every born again believer NOW! Through the course of each chapter, I hope to show how I came to rest in the true grace of our Lord and how he has shown me the life that is ours, not just for the receiving but for the releasing! Since being a pastor for many years, I have preached, taught, and counseled a countless number of Christians encouraging them to tap into the abundant life which resides inside them. Many in the church today have made their way to the cross but have never left! Contrary to popular belief, life is not at the cross (I will share more on this in another section)! True abundant life is in Jesus Christ alone. True abundant living is found by releasing his life from within.

Why abide at a place, the cross, where our Lord himself refused to abide; he chose to die there, not live there, so why should we? The cross and the tomb are both empty. The angel spoke very sobering words to the women who came to the tomb that day expecting to find Jesus: "Why seek ye the living among the dead? He is not here, but is risen" (Luke 24: 5–6 KJV). These words still ring true today: HE IS RISEN INDEED!

Introduction

> According as his divine power hath given unto us all things that pertain unto life and godliness, through the knowledge of him that hath called us to glory and virtue. (2 Peter 1:3 KJV)

We, through Jesus Christ, were given EVERYTHING that pertains to life and godliness. That's good news! It isn't anything that we must work to achieve, fast to attain, or pay to receive. How can the Gospel possibly be good news if we constantly have to work, fast, pay, and pray to please God? It can't! Yet that seems to be the message today in many, if not most assemblies. Paul wrote in Hebrews 11:6 (KJV), "But without faith, it is impossible to please him: for he that cometh to God must believe that he is and that he is a rewarder of them that diligently seek him."

Did you know that the word *please* in this verse means to fully agree? (Strong's Hebrew/Greek G2101). In essence, Paul is saying that without faith, it is impossible to fully agree with God. Agree with God about what? That he is a rewarder of them that work hard for the Lord? Or that he is a rewarder of them that pay a certain percentage to the church? Or that he is a rewarder of them that go to church regularly or fast often? The list could go on and on, but Paul is saying that faith in Jesus is the only way to fully agree with God! By faith in Jesus, he is saying that we must fully agree that what Jesus did for us was enough!

Religion taught me that as a Christian, I had to bear sin, guilt, condemnation, sickness, disease, poverty, and the curse of which God never intends for us to bear (Jesus bore them as our substitute)!

God has established, by His Son, a glorious plan called *the Gospel* (good news). By empowering the church with His Spirit, it can NOW express the Gospel of Christ in His fullness by *demonstrating* the demise of Satan through abundant living. We must now see and understand through Satan's impeachment that he has been relieved of all authority and power, for there has been a paradigm shift of all authority and power by the death, burial, and resurrection of our Lord Jesus Christ.

> And Jesus came and spake unto them saying, all power is given unto me in heaven and in earth (i.e., God gave Jesus the power to bring heaven to earth)! (Matthew 28:18 KJV)

Now that we see Satan for whom he is, we can see ourselves for who we are by fulfilling these teachings:

> Yet thou (Satan) shalt be brought down to hell, to the sides of the pit. They (the church) that see thee shall narrowly look upon thee and consider (understand) thee, saying, is this the man that made the earth to tremble, that did shake the kingdoms; That made the world as a wilderness and destroyed the cities thereof; that opened not the house of his prisoners? (Isaiah 14:15–17 KJV)

> The Spirit of the Lord God is upon me [Jesus]; because the Lord hath anointed me to preach good tidings [(gospel)] unto the meek; he hath sent me to bind up the brokenhearted, to proclaim liberty to the captives, and the opening of the prison to them that are bound: To proclaim the acceptable year [(favorable time)] of the LORD. (Isaiah 61: 1-2 KJV)

The favorable time is—NOW!

This is a book about breaking free from what I call a *religious mentality*, which as a whole, has restricted the movement of the New Testament church. This restriction has not stopped the movement of the church but has restricted it by establishing boundaries and limitations (rules and regulations), causing complete freedom in Christ not to be achieved (we will talk more on this later). I am convinced the Gospel message is not being preached in many New Testament churches across America today because of this mentality. I feel I can be somewhat authoritative because of my religious mindset, which I had succumbed to for so long.

Religious mindset is the term used because people, in general, believe Jesus come to establish a religion. Jesus spoke of a *relationship* not a *religion-ship* with His Father that could only be achieved by an *internal response* not to the cross, but to the *finished work of the cross* (there is a difference) and the resurrection of our Lord from the grave. By *receiving* what Jesus has already accomplished for us, we can, as of today, begin our journey to enjoying everlasting freedom in Christ by understanding who Jesus is and equally important who we are!

Whether believed or not, God's total reason for existing centers solely upon you! God accomplished everything He did from creation with you in mind; from the birth of his son to the death, to the resurrection, and the ascension of his Son, it all resonates around YOU.

CHAPTER 1

Religion-ship

Often, words litigate rather than liberate the believer. The believer should understand and grasp the knowledge of the word religion, to help better understand what religion is and is not. To set the tone for this book, I will explain in more detail what I mean when referring to religion, religious mindsets, and religious mentalities.

Webster defines the word religion as meaning: a belief in the being and perfections of God, in the revelation of his will to man, in man's obligation to obey his commands, in a state of reward and punishment, and in man's accountableness to God; true godliness or piety of life, with the practice of all moral duties. I consider this a very sober and accurate definition of religion. Understand me when I say that I believe in the being and perfections of God, the revelations of his will, and in man's accountableness to God. But the problem I have with religion is that its primary focus is outward, not inward!

Religion directs our attention mainly to our performance rather than Jesus' performance. Not one statement in this definition of religion even remotely mentions God living in us! It is no difference in the keeping of the Old Testament law! It primarily focuses on one's external performance in hopes of holding on to one's eternal position. It seems to direct attention more toward what we do rather than what he did! In its Latin form, the word *religion* means (*re-* "back" + *ligare-* "to bind"). So religion, in its simplest form, means to bind again! Jesus did not come and die to exchange one set of rules and regulations for another set of rules and regulations or bind again.

Furthermore, Jesus did not come to make sure we carried out these religious obligations and then punish us if we did not. However, he did come to carry out the obligations and face punishment because we could not. "Think not that I am come to destroy the law or the prophets: I am not come to destroy, but to fulfill" (Matthew 5:17).

Fulfill means "to satisfy" (Strong's Greek/Hebrew G4137). The Old Testament laws had to be satisfied, and man could not do it. They could not keep these religious laws then, nor can we keep them today.

Jesus came to satisfy outward religion and to re-establish the relationship between God and man. The angel of the Lord spoke to Joseph, the husband of Mary, in a dream, saying:

> Joseph, thou son of David, fear not to take unto thee Mary thy wife: for that which is conceived in her is of the Holy Ghost. And she shall bring forth a son, and thou shalt call his name Jesus: for he shall save his people from their sins. Now all this was done, that it might be fulfilled which was spoken of the Lord by the prophet, saying, Behold, a virgin shall be with child, and shall bring forth a son, and they shall call his name Emmanuel, which being interpreted is, God with us. (Matthew 1:20–23 KJV)

Emmanuel

Understanding the name *Emmanuel* is the key to understanding why Jesus satisfied religion and established relationship.

Emmanuel means "God with us." The word *with* is the Greek word *meta* (Strong's Greek/Hebrew G3326), which means "accompaniment, amid, and within." What this literally means is God came to dwell in, to accompany, to surround, to encompass, and to envelop us, for the purpose of participation. God wants to participate IN our life. This defines relationship! God's purpose wasn't to come to earth in the form of his son, die a hideous death on a cross, raise from the grave, ascend to heaven, then leave us a list of do's and don'ts. If you do this, you can go to heaven; if you don't, you go to hell. That is religion! He came to live within us (our innermost being), accompany us, and participate in our lives. We truly cannot call him Emmanuel until we *let him in*!

What is interesting to note is the name *Emmanuel*. In Hebrew, it is a compound word that denotes our equality with God (Strong's Hebrew/Greek H5973 and H410). It literally means "equal with God"! That is worth repeating again: WE ARE EQUAL WITH GOD! This is God's report; should we not believe the report of the Lord?

How important is it that we see ourselves and speak of ourselves the same way he sees us and speaks of us? We are just as much a son of God and equal with him as Jesus is! Jesus makes us this way! Paul referred to this in the following passage: "Let this mind be in you which was also in Christ Jesus: Who being in the form of God, thought it not robbery to be equal with God" (Philippians 2:5–6 KJV). Permit and allow your mind to become as his by accepting your equality with God!

A religion that focuses solely on our performance rather than our position is a religion that Jesus came to debunk. Religion is nothing more than ceremonial observances of ordinances that call attention to our right doing rather than our right being:

"For the law made nothing perfect, [doing the law does not make you right], but the bringing in of a better hope did [makes us perfect]; by the which we draw nigh unto God" (Hebrews 7:19 KJV). The word for *perfect* is the Greek word *teleioo*, which means "to bring to completion, to finish, accomplish, and to consummate" (Strong's Greek/Hebrew G5048).

Once we receive the *better hope* that this passage is referring to (being born again through Jesus Christ,) then we have instantly been perfected, completed, finished, accomplished, and consummated in our spirit man—that is the way you draw nigh to God. "Draw nigh" means to "*approach* God."

> Jesus saith unto him, I am the way, the truth, and the life: no man cometh unto the Father but by me. (John 14:6 KJV)

We approach God by Jesus Christ alone. That is the only way we can ever approach him. Now that we are in Christ and knowing we are perfect, complete, finished, accomplished, and consummated in him, we must stop TRYING to be all these things by our performance and accept that we are now all these things by his; that is what relationship means! You are now a relative of God. For eternity, he is your Father, and you are his child!

CHAPTER 2

Relationship

The way you are born into your earthly family is the same way you are born into your heavenly family—by seed: "Being born again, not of corruptible seed, but of incorruptible [seed], by the word of God which liveth and abideth forever" (1 Peter 1:23 KJV).

Everything produces after its kind through seed. This also includes man: "So God created man in his own image, in the image of God created he him; male and female created he them. And God blessed them and God said unto them, be fruitful, and multiply, and replenish the earth"(Genesis 1:27–28). Everything was designed by God to reproduce after its kind for the purpose of replenishing or filling up the Earth. God wanted the earth full of people with the same nature as himself.

God did not change his mind or back away from this mandate! However, Genesis chapter three teaches the fall of man and how he, through that one act of disobedience, forfeited the nature of God in his life and took on the nature of Satan, thereby losing his kinship.

Kin-ship

Remember, our intent is not to focus on the fall of man, but the rise of man through Jesus Christ! This is why a greater understanding of the word relationship is so important to the Christian.

Webster defines the word *relationship* as "the state of being related by kindred, affinity, or other alliance." *Kindred* is the word we will be focusing on here to help us understand our relationship—or as I sometimes call it, our *relative-ship*.

The word *kindred* means "to be relatives by blood or marriage; to connect in kind by having the same nature and properties." It is synonymous with the word *relative*. God did not establish a plan to free us from being eternally lost and separate from him; he wanted the man to become like him. He wanted kinship; he wanted children—he wanted a family!

Scripture indications of how at one time, we were of no relation to God; but now through Jesus Christ, we can become his children, "But now in Christ Jesus ye who sometimes were far off are made nigh by the blood of Jesus" (Ephesians 2:13 KJV). The Greek word for *blood* here is the word *aima*, which implies *kindred* (Strong's Greek/Hebrew G129). God saw us as kindred long before we saw him as Father. The forgiveness of sin was given to every person on Earth. The blood of Jesus accomplished this: "In whom we have redemption through his blood, even the forgiveness of sins" (Colossians 1:14). The word *we* implies everyone, not just Christians, EVERYONE! God sees everyone on earth as his child! He sees everyone on earth forgiven! This is implied again, "And he is the propitiation for our sins: and not for ours only, but also for the sins of the whole world" (1 John 2:2).

Activation

For everyone on earth to become his children and for everyone on earth to activate the forgiveness that is already ours, everyone must awaken unto Jesus's complete work of the cross. Isaiah prophesied of this:

> And in that day thou shalt say, O Lord I will praise thee: though thou wast angry with me, thine anger is turned away, and thou comfortedst me. Behold, God is my salvation; I will trust, and not be afraid: for the Lord Jehovah is my strength and my song; he also is my salvation. (Isaiah 12:1–2 KJV)

Receiving what has already been reserved for us is like receiving a new credit card in the mail. It already has the amount reserved in your name, but you cannot access it until YOU activate the card. God, by his grace, has prepared and reserved our purpose and destiny but has given us the responsibility by activating it. Activation takes place by being born again and then by faith in him; you have immediate access provided.

Therefore being justified by faith, we have peace with God through our Lord Jesus Christ, "By whom also we have access by faith into this grace wherein we stand, and rejoice in hope of the glory of God" (Romans 5:1–2 KJV).

We need to understand that believing this doesn't make it true. It's already true. We just need to believe it!

CHAPTER 3

Freedom

Often we sing songs of freedom in our assembly today, yet we are still bound by our consciousness of sin rather than our consciousness of the payment for our sin. Hebrews 10 teaches that the old-covenant sacrifices could never take away sin, and they served as a constant reminder of their sinfulness every year. Verse two states that if these sacrifices were sufficient, then there would be no more conscience of sin:

Hebrews 10:2 (KJV) reads, "For then would they not have ceased to be offered? because that the worshippers once purged should have had no more conscience of sins."

The word *conscience* here means "to become aware" (Strong's Greek/Hebrew G4894). The more conscious or aware we are of sin, the more sin is going to control us. The more consciously aware we are of what Jesus accomplished for us at the cross, the more freedom we experience.

Jesus spoke of freedom in John 8:31–32 as being the point reached by continuing in His Word, "Then said Jesus to those Jews which believed on him, if ye continue in my word, then are ye my disciples indeed; And ye shall know the truth, and the truth shall make you free" (John 8:31–32 KJV).

As I read these passages over and over several times, it became apparent to me that Jesus was talking to believers by this introduction: "Then said Jesus to those Jews which believed on him" (John 8:31 KJV).

They believed in him, yet the implication was they still were not free. Why weren't these *believers* free? They were believers! All believers should be free, should they not? What bound them? I fully understand the statements Jesus made were before the Crucifixion, yet he was making a valid point for life after the cross, which he emphasized to his disciples "continue in my word…you shall know the truth…the truth shall make you free" (John 8:32 KJV).

What bound the believing Jews of that day is the same thing that binds a believer today—PERFORMANCE! The believing Jew of that day still believed that they had to adhere to the Old Covenant rituals of keeping the law along with their acceptance of Christ to be free. This was not the truth then, nor is it the truth now!

Jesus pointed to truth as the ultimate for freedom and that knowing the truth in *him* was the only factor that would bring lasting freedom.

Webster defines *freedom* as "the state or quality of being free; exemption or liberation from the control of some other person or some arbitrary power; liberty." Jesus did this! He fulfilled the requirements of the law for our lasting freedom, and now in him we are truly free and exempt from the demands of the law that bound us to a consciousness of sin.

God desires to teach and educate the believer on how to express the power from within that has been lying dormant in many believers since they were born again. God desires us to be FREE! In Christ, we are FREE! We must stop waiting on God to do something that will make us free. When in truth, he has already done it! He is waiting for us to walk in it! We have it; many of us are unaware because we are not continuing in his Word! Continuing in his word doesn't mean I must read it 24-7. It means I must continue believing what his word declares about me! When He says I am free, I am free!

I ponder over the lack of enthusiasm the church has for freedom. Enthusiasm is one thing the church should never lack. Webster defines enthusiasm as the Greek word *en theos*, which means: possessed by God, infused with a divine spirit, or the God within. We should be enthusiastic about who we are in Christ Jesus and become the church in every sense of the word, "And hath put all things under his feet, and gave him to be head over all things to the church, which is his body, the fulness of him that filleth all in all" (Ephesians 1:22–23 KJV).

I'm not as concerned about people *coming* to church as I am people *becoming* the church!

God, through his son Jesus Christ, has redeemed us from the control of Satan as taught in this passage:

> What? Know ye not that your body is the temple of the Holy Ghost, which is in you, which ye have of God, and ye are not your own? For ye are bought with a price: therefore glorify God in your body, and in your spirit, which are God's. (I Corinthians 6:19–20 KJV)

The word *price* in this passage means to place value on, to esteem (especially of the highest degree). It also means money paid for a thing.

Paul was saying that the price paid for us was determined by the value God placed on us. It's like owning a house that's worth a million dollars. If you decided to sell the house, the price you placed on the house is determined by the worth of the house. God valued you to the highest degree! We know this by God paying the highest price he could ever pay, which was the death of his Son.

Although we may understand the price Jesus paid for our freedom, we present an injustice to him and God when, as believers, we remain bound. Jesus, being the flesh of God, sacrificed everything at the cross for our total freedom so we could glorify God in our body and our spirit.

CHAPTER 4

The Cross

The cross is the most preached about subject of the Bible and rightly so. I want to be careful not to be offensive when speaking of the cross, but at the same time, I hope to broaden one's perspective of the purpose of the cross. For it was there that Jesus died not only for us but as us.

Jesus represented us in death so we could represent him in *life*. Now as his *representatives of life* on earth, he has released us into total freedom not to be suppressed but expressed to the world by fulfilling our purpose and destiny in him. He represented us in death on earth so we could represent him in life on earth!

The very place that Jesus carried our sin, sickness, disease, condemnation, curse, and poverty too is the very place we as his children are to visit but not live! As I stated earlier in this book, the cross was the place to die but not the place to live!

The Attraction and Distraction

The cross is the attraction for lost humanity. For it was there that all humanity was judged: "And I, if I be lifted up from the earth, will draw all men unto me. This he said, signifying what death he should die" (John 12:32–33 KJV). The cross was the instrument of capital punishment used by the government of that day to punish by death any malefactor worthy of death. Although its purpose was and is to draw the lost to the place of the new birth, we must be careful that the cross does not become a distraction to us after we have been born again and made free. (Please hear me out before you judge me a heretic.) Remember, the cross was the instrument of capital punishment used by the government of that day to punish by death any malefactor considered worthy of death.

Suppose you are on death row for a crime that you committed that is worthy of death. The day arrives in which the guard comes to take you to your execution death by the electric chair. The guard proceeds to strap you into the chair, strategically placing and buckling every strap around the specific parts of your body, fixating you to the chair, which will send hundreds of volts of electricity coursing through your whole body, killing you almost instantly. This paints an ugly picture but only to make a very valid point.

Just before the guard pulls the switch, the phone rings. The voice on the other end of the phone says, "Release him, for he has been declared not guilty." The guard begins the procedure of unbuckling the straps that bind you to the chair. Once released, you are free to go. Elated by your *newfound* freedom, you leave the place of punishment and death. You are FREE! You don't hang around that place of death anymore. Nor do you argue with the warden by saying you are guilty. You go on to enjoy your new freedom by living life to the fullest. It is the same with the cross! In the same manner, Jesus, through his death on the cross, has declared you NOT GUILTY! In John 10:27 (KJV), Jesus said, "My sheep hear my voice, and I know them, and they follow me." The word *voice* is the Greek word *phone*

(Strong's Greek/Hebrew G5456). The voice on the phone has declared you NOT GUILTY! You are FREE!

Paul further explains this great exchange: "You know that our Lord Jesus Christ was kind enough to give up all His riches and become poor, so that you could become rich" (2 Corinthians 8:9 CEV).

The Transfer of Power from Heaven to Earth

> For the preaching of the cross is to them that perish foolishness; but unto us which are saved it is the power of God. (1 Corinthians 1:18 KJV)

The cross was the instrument used by God to begin the transfer of his power from heaven (God) to earth (man).

The word power in this verse is a Greek word *dunimas*. (Strong's Hebrew/Greek G1411) Dunimas power means the inherent ability residing in a thing by virtue of its nature. Man's nature became sinful by virtue of Adam's act of disobedience. Because of this, the power and ability of sin became inherent, causing Adam's sinful nature to pass from generation to generation. Jesus, however, as the Son of God, having the same nature of God, through his inherent power destroyed by his death on the cross, Satan and his stronghold of sin which he had on mankind. Paul explains it this way, "For if when we were enemies, we were reconciled to God by the death of his son, much more, being reconciled, we shall be saved by his life" (Romans 5:10 KJV). The word *reconciled* means "to change mutually or; share in common" (Strong's Hebrew/Greek2644).

Mutual Change

Through Jesus's death on the cross, there was a mutual change (exchange) that took place. He took on our sin nature and in turn, he allowed us to take on his God (divine) nature. Paul explains, "Knowing this, that our old man [the sin nature] is crucified with him, that the body of sin might be destroyed, that henceforth we should not serve sin" (Romans 6:6 KJV). The word *destroyed* in this passage is the Greek word *Kat-arg-eh-o*, which means "to loosen and render entirely useless, idle, void, and of none effect (Strong's Hebrew/Greek 2673).

The same word for destroyed is found in Hebrews 2:14 (KJV), "Forasmuch then as the children are partakers of flesh and blood, he also himself likewise took part of the same; that through death he might destroy him that had the power of death, that is the devil." Jesus's death on the cross destroyed the devil! Let me write this again so no one will think this is a misprint—Jesus's death on the cross destroyed the devil! He is alive only to those that will give him life! Jesus forced Satan to loosen his power over man by rendering him useless, idle, void, and of none effect. The devil is not a problem anymore to those that know this!

In 1 Peter 5:8–9 (KJV), Peter tells us, "to be sober, be vigilant because your adversary the devil, as a roaring lion, walketh about, seeking whom he may devour. Whom resist steadfast in the faith." Those who do not know the devil is destroyed can be devoured by him. He renders no power and poses no threat to all that know and trust what Jesus has accomplished at the cross!

No More Strong Man

> When a strong man armed keepeth his palace, his goods are in peace: But when a stronger than he shall come upon him, and overcome him, he taketh from him all his armour wherein he trusted, and divided his spoils. (Luke 11:21–22 KJV)

That is what Jesus accomplished for us at the cross! The strong man (Satan) had everything going for him. He guarded what he claimed as his without any conflict. When the stronger than he appeared (Jesus), he *overcame* him, loosened his hold, rendered him useless, void, and of none effect by taking from him all of his *armor* (instruments of war). Notice how Matthew explains it: "Or else how can one enter into a strong man's house, and spoil his goods, except he first bind the strong man? And then he will spoil his house" (Matthew 12:29 KJV).

The Strong Man's House

The strong man's house is referring to humankind. Satan set up house within humankind due to Adam's one act of disobedience. Jesus, by taking our sinful nature to the cross and putting it to death, gives all that accept him, his divine nature. This is the great exchange! Paul explains this in Romans 5:19 (KJV), "For as by one man's disobedience [Adam] many were made sinners, so by the obedience of one [Jesus] shall many be made righteous." The focus is no longer on the strong man; the focus is now on the *stronger than he*. When we take up the cross and follow Jesus, we accept all that Jesus accomplished at the cross so we can enjoy life more abundantly, thereby rendering the devil of no use, void, and none effect in our life!

Taking Up the Cross

Throughout three of the four Gospels, Jesus spoke of taking up the cross and following him:

> And he that taketh not his cross, and followeth after me, is not worthy of me.: ...whosoever will come after me, let him deny himself, and take up his cross, and follow me....take up the cross and follow me. ...if any man will come after me, let him deny himself, and take up his cross daily, and follow me. (Matthew 10:38; Mark 8:34, Mark 10:21; Luke 9:23 KJV)

> To take up the cross that Jesus referred to in these passages means to accept the mutual change of natures. (Matthew 10:38; Mark 8:34; Mark 10:21; Luke 9:23 KJV)

The word *taketh* means to accept, and to receive (Strong's Hebrew/Greek G2983). As our substitute, Jesus willingly, through his love for us, accepted and received our sin nature, knowing that by doing so, it would take him to the cross. All that our sin nature could focus on was sin which included condemnation, sickness, disease, poverty, etc. To be made worthy, we must willingly accept and receive his divine nature which focuses on abundant living (i.e., love, victory, health, joy, peace, hope, etc.).

JERRY ROBINSON

Our Substitute

When the meaning of the word *substitute* became a realization to me, strongholds due to erroneous teachings began to crumble. *Webster's* 1828 edition dictionary defines the word *substitute* as "one person put in place of another to answer the same purpose; a person with full powers to act for another in an office." That is exactly what our Lord did for us! He received full authority and power, by His Father, to become our substitute in representing us by drawing the whole of lost humanity with its sinful nature to the cross, so we with His divine nature could, in turn, carry the whole of His salvation to the world!

When Jesus died on the cross, it was like each of us dying because he died in our place as our substitute. In the same respect, when Jesus rose from the grave it is like each of us has risen from the grave because he rose from the grave as our substitute. Do you get the picture? When we received Jesus as our personal Lord and Savior we activated the crucifixion with Christ that took place over two thousand years ago. Galatians 2:20 (KJV) reads, "I am crucified with Christ: nevertheless I live; yet not I, but Christ liveth in me: and the life which I now live in the flesh I live by the faith of the Son of God who loved me, and gave Himself for me."

Let me clarify our crucifixion with Christ. We were not crucified with Christ the moment we were born again as some teach today; neither do we crucify ourselves over and over again as some teach we must do to live this Christian life. The New Testament teachings of Paul teach us we were crucified, already, with Christ! Our crucifixion took place when his did! We activate this crucifixion by receiving by *faith* what Jesus accomplished for us over two thousand years ago. Our faith does not move us to crucify our flesh. Our faith moves us into the place where the flesh has already been crucified. Christ is that place!

Judgment Seat

John 12:32–33 (KJV) states, "And I, if I be lifted up from the earth, will draw all men unto me. This he said, signifying what death he should die."

At the beginning of this chapter, I used these passages to make a valid point concerning the cross. Now let us look at the preceding passage to help give us more clarity to what Jesus was saying:

> Now is the judgment of this world: now shall the prince of this world be cast out. (John 12:31 KJV)

Wouldn't it be good news if the judgment was completely completed at the cross and that there actually wasn't another judgment after death for us the church? I was taught most of my life that after we die, we as Christians will stand before God and be judged according to what we've done in this life whether good or bad. The scripture that is used to supposedly promote this point is found in the book of 2 Corinthians:

> For we must all appear before the judgment seat of Christ; that everyone may receive the things done in his body, according to that he hath done, whether it be good or bad. (2 Cor. 5:10 KJV)

For the life of me, I cannot imagine why Jesus would die on the cross as judgment for our sin and then after we die judge us again for the same crimes! That does not sound like good news to me. But it must be true for this passage of scripture says so. Or does it? Let us take a more in-depth look at this passage and what Paul was actually saying. First, he says that we must all appear before the judgment seat of Christ.

Many teach this passage as a throne positioned in heaven where Jesus will sit and judge the church according to what we have done while alive on earth and that we will stand before him at that heavenly throne where he will recall to our attention all the good and bad that we have ever done throughout our lives while living on earth. Let us break down some of the key words found in this passage in hopes of a better understanding of what Paul was saying. The word *bad* is the Greek word *KaK-os'*, which means "evil, harm, ill, and wicked" (*Strong's Hebrew/Greek G2556*). So in essence, many would have us believe that Jesus is going to make us stand before him in the heavenly realm and bring before us all the evil, harm, ill will, and wickedness (*which by the way constitutes as sin*) that we've ever done? Is that good news? *Absolutely NOT!* Neither is Jesus going to bring before us the *good* that we have done. But what is the good Paul is referring to? Let us understand that good is just as bad as bad when one thinks that our good will help us gain access to heaven. Look what Jesus says:

> Many will say to me in that day, Lord, Lord, have we not prophesied in thy name? And in thy name have cast out devils? And in thy name done many wonderful *(good)* works? And then will I profess unto them, I never knew you: depart from me, ye that work iniquity. (Matt. 7:22–23 KJV)

Jesus is saying in this passage that these guys were trusting in their good works for righteousness rather than trusting in Jesus's good works for righteousness. Therefore, he says depart from me, ye that work iniquity (*sin*). This passage is saying that good and bad are rewarded as the same when one puts confidence in their performance (*Old Covenant*) rather than Jesus's performance (*New Covenant*). Furthermore, Paul writes in Hebrews that the covenant that found fault in people (*Old Covenant*) was about to vanish away and be replaced by a New Covenant:

> For finding fault with them, he saith, Behold, the days come, saith the Lord, when I will make a new covenant with the house of Israel and with the house of Judah. (Heb. 8:8 KJV)

> For I will be merciful to their unrighteousness, and their sins and their iniquities will I REMEMBER no more. (Heb. 8:12 KJV; *emphasis on* remember *mine*)

Paul is saying that in this new covenant, God plans to be merciful to our unrighteousness and our sins he will *remember* no more, which literally means he will never connect our sin to us again! *NEVER!* That's good news!

Besides, in most all of Paul's epistles, he always started his letters by saying grace and peace from God our Father and the Lord Jesus Christ. How can we live with peace in our hearts if we believe we will be judged at the end of this life for all the bad we have ever done? We can't!

So What Is the Judgment Seat of Christ?

Please allow me to stretch your mind for a moment and give you something to ponder on. What if the judgment seat of Christ was a past event, not a future event as many teach? What if the judgment seat of Christ is where Christ himself took all our sins upon himself at an elevated place called Calvary where the cross was erected and judgment was carried out to the fullest! Let me explain.

The word *seat* in this passage does not refer to a heavenly throne as some teach. *Seat* means "an elevated place." It is an official seat of a judge or place where judgment is meted out on earth, but never does it refer to a heavenly throne.

This word *seat* is the Greek word *bema* (*Strong's Hebrew/Greek G968*). Although this word is used many times throughout the scriptures, only once is it translated as a throne and this is found in Acts 12:21 when speaking of King Herod as he sat upon his earthly throne or platform or elevated place.

> And upon a set day Herod, arrayed in royal apparel, sat upon his throne [*seat*] and made an oration unto them. (Acts 12:21 KJV)

I'm convinced that the judgment seat of Christ was an elevated place on earth (*Calvary*), not heaven where the official Judge of all judges was carried to the cross to execute judgment in the earth as the Son of Man. John explained it this way:

> Verily, verily, I say unto you, He that heareth my word, and believeth on him that sent me, hath everlasting life and shall not come into *condemnation*; but is passed from death unto

life. For as the Father hath life in himself; so hath he given to the Son to have life in himself. And hath given him authority to execute *judgment* also because he is the Son of man. (John 5:24, 26, 27 KJV)

The word *condemnation* in verse 24 is the same word as *judgment* in verse 27 (*Strong's Hebrew/Greek G2920*). In essence, Jesus was saying that all who believe in him shall *NOT* come into judgment but life! It was Jesus who went into judgment on the cross as our substitute so we could go into life! We can never come into judgment before God again! Why? Because Jesus entered into condemnation so we would never have to again! Isn't that good news!

Now let me go back to John 12:31 and expound further: Now is the judgment of this world: now shall the prince of this world be cast out (John 12:31 KJV).

Notice Jesus says, "Now is the judgment of this world." So the subject matter of this verse is "judgment" and the time is NOW! Then he says, "Now shall the prince of this world be cast out." The subject matter in this part of the verse is the "prince of this world being cast out," and the time is NOW! When Jesus took all our judgment upon himself, the prince of this world (*Satan*) lost all his rights and privileges toward us. Look what John says about this in the book of Revelation.

And I heard a loud voice saying in heaven, Now is come salvation, and strength, and the kingdom of our God, and the power of his Christ: for the accuser [*Satan*] of our brethren is cast down [*out*], *which* accused them before our God day and night. (Rev. 12:10 KJV)

This is not a future event, this is a past event! This passage was fulfilled at the cross. That's good news!

Now that we understand John 12:31 we can better understand verses 32–33 which explain how Jesus is going to and *did* make all this happen.

> And I, if I be lifted up from the earth, will draw all men unto me. This he said, signifying what death he should die. (John 12:32–33 KJV)

The words "lifted up" means to *elevate* (*Strong's Hebrew/Greek G5312*). The statement "signifying what death he should die" refers to Jesus's death on the cross. Jesus was lifted up (*elevated*) on a cross at a place called Calvary where he drew ALL judgment unto himself. All means ALL!

Often I would think about and dread the day that I must stand before God at the judgment seat of Christ to be judged for all I've ever done or didn't do while living in this earthly body. Now I no longer think about my heavenly Father *ever* judging me for all the wrong I have ever done for through Jesus he already has. Now I simply thank my heavenly Father for placing all judgment for sin upon his son Jesus so I can enjoy abundant life and peace NOW! This truly is good news!

Let us look at another scripture concerning the judgment seat of Christ.

> But why dost thou judge thy brother? Or why dost thou set at naught thy brother? For we shall all stand before the judgment seat of Christ. For it is written, as I live, saith the Lord, every knee shall bow to me, and every

tongue shall confess to God. (Rom. 14:10–11 KJV)

When reading this passage, one would again assume that we are all going to stand before a throne in heaven where Jesus will be seated. It's at that throne we will be judged according to what we have done while alive on earth. Again, this is a past experience, not a future one. But take notice to what Paul says in verse 11, "For it is written, as I live, saith the Lord, every knee shall bow to me, and every tongue shall confess to God." Just what are we going to confess? Are we to confess all the bad we've ever done? Are we to confess all the good we've ever done? Let us allow scripture to answer scripture. Look what Paul writes in Philippians.

> Wherefore God also hath highly exalted him, and given him a name which is above every name: That at the name of Jesus every knee should bow, of things in heaven, and things in earth, and things under the earth; And that every tongue should confess that Jesus Christ is Lord, to the glory of God the Father. (Phil. 2:9–11 KJV)

Do you now see who we will bow to and confess to and oh by the way as Paul writes what we shall confess? *"That Jesus Christ is Lord!"* Confessing all the bad we have ever done or all the good we have ever done does not bring glory to God the Father. What brings glory to God our Father is confessing Jesus! I boldly do this today! I'm not waiting until some futuristic day to be judged because I know I already have been judged at Calvary. That's good news!

Boldness in the Day of Judgment

First John 4:17 (KJV) says, "Herein is our love made perfect, that we may have boldness in the Day of Judgment: because as he is, so are we in this world."

By using the latter part of this verse in a previous chapter, I stated that once we're born again, we become just like Jesus in reference to our spirit; and that this is exactly how our heavenly Father sees us. Yet many take the first part of this passage to mean a future judgment for the church and not a past one. The day of judgment is the same event as the judgment seat of Christ that Paul alluded to in the previous passages. The day of judgment, referring to Jesus's sacrificial death on the cross, displayed such a wonderful, powerful, and perfect love of God toward man that it should instill within us a confidence that we can walk and abide in the boldness of who we are in Christ at all times. But sadly, I have counseled with scores of Christians that spend most of their Christian lives condemning themselves for bad things they did or good things they should have done but failed to do (*I have just described every Christian*) and rightly so for when one believes that we are going to be judged in the future for all the good and bad we've ever done, it does not nor will not instill confidence or boldness within one's heart.

> And hereby we know that we are of the truth, and shall assure our hearts before him. For if our heart condemn us, God is greater than our heart, and knoweth all things. Beloved, if our heart condemn us not, then have we confidence toward God. (1 John 3:19–21 KJV)

We must know and understand that the way we ensure our hearts is by accepting that Jesus was the final judgment for our transgressions. King David referred to this when he penned these words:

> As far as the east is from the west, so far hath he removed our transgressions from us. (Ps. 103:12 KJV)

But what about Hebrews 9:24–28?

Let me make one more observation concerning judgment and its completion.

Many people look at Hebrews 9:24–28 and declare that a judgment after death for the church is imminent. The truth is that these passages say right the opposite. Let us look at these scriptures.

> For Christ is not entered into the holy places made with hands, which are the figures of the true; but into heaven itself, now to appear in the presence of God for us: Nor yet that he should offer himself often, as the high priest entereth into the holy place every year with blood of others; For then must he often have suffered since the foundation of the world: but now once in the end of the world hath he appeared to put away sin by the sacrifice of himself. And as it is appointed unto men once to die, but after this the judgment: So Christ was once offered to bear the sins of many; and unto them that look for him shall he appear the second time without sin unto salvation. (Heb. 9:24–28 KJV)

Notice Paul says that Jesus didn't enter into the tabernacle of the Old Covenant but into heaven itself to appear in the presence of God for us. He goes on to say that he should not enter into the holy place often to offer himself as the high priest of the Old Covenant did where they took blood sacrifices into the holy place regularly. He says but ONCE at the end of the world has, he appeared to put away sin by the sacrifice of himself. (*World* is the Greek word *aion*, which means "age" [*Strong's Greek/Hebrew G165*].) The term "end of the world" (age) is referring to the end of the Old Covenant age, not the end of planet earth as some might think. Jesus's death, burial, and resurrection brought about the close of the Old Covenant age to usher in a New Covenant age. The next part of this passage is very important: and as it is appointed unto men ONCE *(emphasis on once mine)* to die, but after this the judgment, so Christ was ONCE offered to bear the sins of many. Did you catch that? The appointment to die was Jesus's appointment, not ours, for we were already dead spiritually. The appointment for judgment was Jesus's appointment as well. The word *man* is the Greek word *anthropos* (*Strong's Greek/Hebrew G444*), which means "a human being, a certain man"—not just any human being and any man but a CERTAIN MAN. The human being, the certain man whom Paul is referring to, is Jesus. He died for us, was judged for us, was raised for us and now appears in the presence of God for us. He is not in the presence of God pleading our case when we blow it for he did that at the cross. That is why Paul says that unto them that look for him shall he appear the second time without sin. Please understand that the first time he came it was because of sin that separated our spirit from God. The second time he came (*and he did come a second time. Read Acts 2*) it was to bring complete and total salvation!

CHAPTER 5

How Can We Escape?

> How shall we escape, if we neglect so great salvation; which at the first began to be spoken by the Lord, and was confirmed unto us by them that heard him. (Hebrews 2:3 KJV)

When Paul spoke the words in Hebrews 2:3, he was indicating that there was a great salvation made available to every person. A great salvation that was spoken, first, to us by our Lord but is to be established by them that hears. Paul writes:

> Wherefore, my beloved, as ye have always obeyed, not as in my presence only, but now much more in my absence, work out your own salvation with fear and trembling; For it is God which worketh in you both to will and to do of his good pleasure. (Philippians 2:12–13 KJV)

The words *work out* in verse twelve mean to accomplish or finish (Strong's Greek/Hebrew G2716). In verse 13, Paul stated: "[that]… it is God which worketh in you both to will and to do of his good pleasure." The word *worketh* means to be efficient or the *causing effect* that causes anything to be what it is (Strong's Greek/Hebrew G1754). What Paul was saying to the church is that the one that worketh this great salvation in us is the same one that will work it out of us! In other words, Paul was saying that what God has already finished and perfected within us; he wants to manifest through us! If we neglect the great salvation that already resides within us, then the result of that neglect with show up outwardly in our lives. How can we escape what the finished work of the cross destroyed if we don't acknowledge and agree with the power of the finished work of the cross that resides within?

> For the preaching of the cross is to them that perish foolishness; but unto us which are saved it is the power of God. (1 Corinthians 1:18 KJV)

Born Again

In many churches across America today, the message of the new birth has been sorely misconceived and misconstrued with the message of salvation. Although one cannot enjoy so great salvation without first being born again, there is a credible difference between the two; thus explaining what Jesus meant when speaking to believers about becoming free. Jesus, speaking to Nicodemus, said in John 3:3 (KJV), "Except a man be born again he cannot see the kingdom of God." In this passage, Jesus was speaking of two different realms, the spiritual and the soulish. When Jesus stated: except a man be born again, He was referring strictly to man's spirit. The spirit of man is the only part of man that can ever be born again. When He said that he could not see the kingdom of God, He was referring to man's soul. (I will explain this in more detail later in another section.)

To be born again simply means as one's spirit being brought into spiritual life by the conception of the Holy Spirit:

> And the angel answered and said unto her, [Mary] The Holy Ghost shall come upon thee, and the power of the Highest shall overshadow thee: therefore also that holy thing which shall be born of thee shall be called the Son of God. (Luke 1:35 KJV)

This is why Jesus said in John 3:6 (KJV), "That which is born of Spirit is spirit (of the Spirit realm)."

Jesus was born from above and into the earth to bring salvation so all, you and I, which are born from above and into the earth, can experience salvation!

Here is something worth noting in the passage: the angel said unto Mary that holy thing born of her shall be called the Son of God. The same holy thing birthed inside of Mary is the same holy thing that birthed inside of you, the believer. In other words, the same thing that made Jesus the Son of God is the same thing that makes you the Son of God. It is at the point of our new birth; we are called *the Son of God*. John referred to this in 1 John 3:1 and 2 (KJV), "We are called sons of God...and... now are we the sons of God." This title is ours by right of birth. That makes you just as much a Son of God as Jesus is! Receive it! Accept it! Confess it!

Salvation

Salvation, on the other hand, has a completely different meaning. It means to rescue, safety, deliver, and health (Strong's Greek/Hebrew G4991). The word salvation derives from the word *save*, which means to deliver, protect, heal, preserve, do well, be whole, and make whole (Strong's Greek/Hebrew G4982). In a sense, one can assume that being born again can mean a type of deliverance, protection, health, wellness, wholeness, etc. As a whole, I see more Christians bound, sick, diseased and broken than ever before. We sing about victory in Jesus but seemingly live day after day defeated. So I must conclude that the new birth alone isn't enough to bring about the rest that Jesus spoke of:

> Come unto me, all ye that labour and are heavy laden and I will give you rest. Take my yoke upon you, and learn of me; for I am meek and lowly in heart: and ye shall find rest unto your souls. For my yoke is easy, and my burden is light. (Matthew 11:28–30 KJV)

When Jesus said, "*I will give you rest,*" he was referring to being born again simply because rest always accompanies the new birth. *Always!* Then Jesus went on to say, "Learn of me… and ye shall find rest unto your souls." That's the salvation part! Our spirit is already at rest and will always be at rest. Now our soul needs to learn this.

In the next chapter, I will explain more concerning the difference between the new birth (*being born again*) and being saved (*salvation*).

CHAPTER 6

The Birth of a New Baby

You are comprised of three parts: spirit, soul, and body. We know this by Paul's reference to man in the following passages in 1 Thessalonians 5:23 and Hebrews 4:12 (KJV):

> I pray God your whole spirit, soul, and body be preserved blameless unto the coming of our Lord Jesus Christ. For the word of God is quick, and powerful, and sharper than any two-edged sword, piercing even to the dividing asunder of soul and spirit, and of the joints and marrow, and is a discerner of the thoughts and intents of the heart. (1 Thessalonians 5:23; Hebrews 4:12 KJV)

Remember, your spirit is the only part of you that can ever be born again. It is the inner man, "that which is born of Spirit is spirit" (John 3:6 KJV). Jesus was teaching Nicodemus salvation gains entrance into one's life with the new birth of our spirit (i.e., the causing effect. Refer back to chapter 5 on the explanation of Philippians 2:13). Spiritually speaking, a new birth has taken place when a person is born again. Their spirit is mature because it has all of God residing within it. They still look the same on the outside as they did before they were born again. They still have the same habits, whether good or bad, as they did before they were born again. The only change that has taken place is to their spirit.

It has been recreated. Second Corinthians 5:17–18 (KJV) reads, "Therefore if any man be in Christ, he is a new creature: old things are passed away; behold, all things are become new. And all things are of God." This is the part I like to emphasize the most—and all things are of God! Everything about your new spirit is of God. The word creature means, creation, or original formation (Strong's Greek/Hebrew G2937). Being born again instantly makes our spirit anew, placing us back into our original formation before the fall. Paul stated that we are a *new* creature in Christ. New means freshness (Strong's Greek/Hebrew G2537). Our spirits are constantly fresh and new in Christ because there is nothing of the old any longer in our spirit. Therefore everything about our spirit is of God! Hallelujah! That's good news!

In John 3:3 (KJV) Jesus said, "Except a man be born again, he cannot see the kingdom of God." The word *see* means "to know, have knowledge, consider, be aware, perceive, understand" (Strong's Greek/Hebrew G1492). Here Jesus is referring to the soul-ish realm. Now the church, being a new creation in Christ in spirit, must endeavor to learn how to renew the soul by teaching it to feed on our born again spirit. Jesus said, "It is the spirit that quickeneth; the flesh profiteth nothing: the words that I speak unto you, they are spirit and they are life" (John 6:63 KJV). Jesus was emphatically saying it is through your spirit life proceeds. If our spirit is dead (dead to God through the fall of Adam), so is everything about us dead. However, if our spirit is alive (born again), then everything about us should be alive because his words that He spoke are spirit and life in our spirit.

Roman 8:16 (KJV) says, "The Spirit itself beareth witness with our spirit, that we are the children of God." Did you notice that Paul did not mention the Spirit bears witness with or testifies to our soul that we are children of God? The Spirit bears witness with our spirit or corroborates with our spirit. We are born of God; therefore, we are children of God! The word *our* in this passage is the Greek word *hemon*, and it means *from us* (Strong's Greek/Hebrew G2257). The Holy Spirit bears witness from our (now) holy spirit. Our spirit is just as holy as God's Spirit simply because His Holy Spirit abides in our newly created spirit, which makes our spirit just as holy as his! Now our holy spirit must, in turn, testify to our soul, declaring who and what we are.

The soul is made of several components that are vital factors in our lives: our mind, will, emotions, intellect, and reasoning.

It is somewhat easy to tell when a Christian is living from their soul being fed from the flesh (carnal) man rather than living from their soul being fed from their born again full of God spirit man. Living from a flesh (carnal) fed soul means being dictated by the mind (i.e., carnal thinking rather than spiritual thinking).

Your will (i.e., doing what your flesh desires rather than what your spirit desires). Your emotions (i.e., allowing your emotions to control you rather than you controlling your emotions). Your intellect and reasoning (i.e., you choose to speculate and draw conclusions without godly wisdom and knowledge of the matter). People who live from their soul, which feeds from the flesh, are often offended, depressed, oppressed, bound, sick, negative, paranoid, insecure, and the list could continue to list many others. These people can be born again believers but still not freed because their soul is still holding to the old things and rejecting the new.

It is like someone I know who recently underwent a liver transplant. The old liver became nonfunctional due to substance abuse and later removed. He received certain medications to take internally so that his body did not reject the new liver by thinking it was the former nonfunctional liver. From the new liver, there began to spring new life! God, through his son, has given each of us an opportunity through the new birth to receive a new spirit to replace the old nonfunctional one due to substance abuse (sin). From the new spirit springs new life! Along with the new spirit, God has also given us a new word (the Gospel) that must be taken internally (mentally) so that we never reject the life that our new spirit has brought us by thinking it is the former nonfunctional one. With this new spirit and a new word, we are empowered to transform our soul and express our new life to the world!

God responded to our sinfulness, by creating an entrance (Jesus Christ) into His kingdom thereby creating new life within us. We respond to God by creating an exit for His life to continue flowing out of us. God designed our spirit to respond to his spirit. Our soul was designed and created to respond to our born again spirit. Because "all things were created by Him, and for him" (Colossians 1:16 KJV), our body was designed and created to manifest the response.

A New Heart

> A new heart also will I give you and a new spirit will I put within you: and I will take away the stony heart out of your flesh, and I will give you a heart of flesh. (Ezekiel 36:26 KJV)

Jesus said, "Thou shalt love the Lord thy God with all thy heart, and with all thy soul, and with all thy mind" (Matthew 22:37 KJV). Even though the heart, the soul, and the mind are closely linked it is hard to distinguish between them. Yet since Jesus referred to each one independently of each other, we must conclude that there is a creditable difference between them. We have explained the makeup of the soul and all that it incorporates, which includes the mind, will, emotions, intellect, reasoning, and personality. The word *mind* in Matthew 22:37 implies the exercise of the imagination through deep thought. I like to refer to it as meditation. It is meditation upon God's word where God speaks to me from my spirit, not heaven as some may think. As we dwell on God's word with our mind through deep thought, it opens the flow of life from our born again spirit (our spirit is full of life for it is full of God) channeling what is in our spirit into our mind. Paul called it renewing our mind in Roman 12:2.

The heart, on the other hand, is defined as the seat or core of feelings and thought. (Strong's Greek/Hebrew G2588) It is where our conscience resides. Proverbs 4:23 (KJV), "Keep thy heart with all diligence; for out of it are the issues of life."

The heart is the center of spiritual activity. It is the place where the spirit and the soul OR the soul and the flesh (whichever WE allow predominance) issue out. In other words, either what gets into the heart comes from the soul-feeding from the heavenly spiritual realm, or it comes from the soul-feeding from the fleshly carnal realm. It is from that abundance that the mouth speaks (or issues out) (Matthew 12:34/Luke 6:45 KJV).

What part does our heart play in our relationship with God? God created a new spirit within us by the new birth, "that which is born of the Spirit is [your] spirit" (John 3:6 KJV). This fulfilled Ezekiel 36:26 instantly in reference to the spirit of man, but fulfilling Ezekiel 36:26 in reference to the heart is an ongoing process. Because of our new spirit, we now have a heart changeable. This passage says "a new heart also will I give you." The word *give* in Hebrew means *assign or appoint* (Hebrew/Greek H5414). In other words, God has assigned and appointed us complete control over our hearts; so what we put there is up to us!

What Is Your Focus

What we focus on we will empower in our lives. Another way to put it is, "What we give our attention to we will give our intention to." In reality, what gets our focus and attention will ultimately get our heart. Proverbs 23:7 (KJV) teaches us this, "For as he thinketh in his heart, so is he." Jesus shared a parable in the Gospels concerning the heart: Matthew 13 (KJV), "Hear ye therefore the parable of the sower." In verse 19, it says, "When any one heareth the word of the kingdom, and understandeth it not, then cometh the wicked one, and catcheth away that which was sown in the heart. This is he which received seed by the wayside." (Greek word for catcheth is *har-pazo*, which means to seize, pluck, pull, take by force, Strong's Greek/Hebrew G726). Correctly understanding this passage is the difference between Christians living a defeated life or Christians living the victorious life that God intended from the beginning of creation. Notice he did not say the wicked one could catch away that which was sown in the spirit. He said he could catch away that which was sown in the heart.

Let me take a moment to perhaps clarify something here. I am convinced that the devil (Satan) was totally defeated through the death, burial, and resurrection of our Lord Jesus Christ. Listen to what Jesus said after his resurrection: "And Jesus came and spake unto them, saying, all power is given unto me in heaven and in earth" (Matthew 28:18 KJV). I believe *all* means *all*! In essence, the devil per se has no power for Jesus has it all. Paul believed that the devil was defeated as well: "Forasmuch then as the children are partakers of flesh and blood, he also likewise took part of the same; that through death he might destroy him that had the power of death, that is, the devil" (Hebrews 2:14 KJV). So when I refer to "the devil," I am referring to wicked thoughts and wicked ideologies that are still prevalent today. The word devil throughout scripture is almost always used as an adjective, not a noun. An adjective describes a person, place, or thing. So I believe the word devil is simply a description of wicked people, wicked places, and wicked things like thoughts, actions, etc. The truth is that although Adam's intentional disobedience (*the devil didn't force him to do it*) caused separation between God and man, Jesus's intentional obedience brought them back into such a glorious union to the point where the spirit of man can *never* be separated from God again! Now that's good news!

Sealed

> In whom ye also trusted, after that ye heard the word of truth, the gospel of your salvation; in whom also after that ye believed, ye were sealed with the Holy Spirit of promise. Which is the earnest of our inheritance until the redemption of the purchased possession, unto the praise of His glory. (Ephesians 1:13–14 KJV)

What was sealed? The word *sealed* is the Greek word *sphargizo*, which means "to secure and preserve." The Holy Spirit seals (i.e., securely preserves) our spirit. Notice that Paul says that the believer is sealed with the Holy Spirit of promise. It is our spirit that has been sealed with this promise. Therefore, NOTHING can catch away what is sown in our born again spirit!

In Luke's Gospel, chapter 8, verse 12 (KJV), he refers to what Matthew calls the *wicked one* as the devil and *that which was sown* as the Word of God. The question we must ask is this: How can the devil take away the word of God sown in our hearts? He cannot! Only by getting us, through deception, to focus our attention on his word rather than God's word can he gain access into our hearts. We must become responsible for the seed that we allow into our hearts. The design of a seed is to produce, whether it is a good seed or a bad seed.

The heart of man is the fertile ground where seed plants and harvests. The harvest is simply the manifestation of the type of seed planted, or in other words, the fruit. Seed can change as quickly as thought changes. Since seeds are words (Luke 8:11/1 Peter 1:23) and words are thoughts not spoken, that is what Jesus meant in Matthew 6:31 (KJV), "Therefore take no thought saying," which proves that thoughts are words. And since Proverbs 23:7 (KJV) teaches that "as a man thinketh in his heart so is he," then we must conclude the only way that a bad seed can gain entrance into our hearts is through the avenue of thought!

Our beliefs create our lives (what we believe is what we will act on because what we act on is what we think on), then we should think on untainted things, right?

Are You Master of Your Thoughts?

> And causing every thought to come under the authority of Christ. (2 Corinthians 10:5 BBE)

We are master of our thoughts, not God, not the devil, not any other person—we are! God designed and created us and placed us in control of our lives that includes our thinking. I am not saying that we cannot be enticed by a deceptive thought. I am saying that as sons of God, we have the authority to replace deceptive thought with inceptive thought. The power of bondage is no longer relevant; therefore, we have the authority to change our thoughts, thereby changing our actions resulting in changing our lives!

CHAPTER 7

We Are of What World?

> They are not of the world, even as I am not of the world. (John 17:16 KJV)

When Jesus made this statement, he was talking to His Heavenly Father concerning the church. Still, what was Jesus saying? The word *of* is a primary preposition that denotes origin (Strong's Greek/Hebrew G1537). Jesus was saying that as born again believers, our origin has changed. We are no longer *of* this world but that our origin now is *of* another world, a heavenly one. The definition of origin is a coming into existence, a beginning, and a birth. That is what Jesus meant when talking to Nicodemus about being born again or born from above (John 3:3). Our origins, our existence, our beginning, and our birth are now from above. Must we begin thinking this way?

When Jesus prayed in John 17:15 that the Father does not take them out of the world but that he keep them from the evil that is in the world, his purposes were twofold. To pray for the protection of the church while in this world and that the church would share of the new world they were of. We must differentiate which world we are of if we are to make a difference in the world we are in.

As He Is, So Are We?

John understood exactly which world he was of when he wrote the words in 1 John 4:17 (KJV), "As he is, so are we in this world." Notice this was not a question but a statement. The church *is* just like Jesus in this world! Wow! What a revelation for the church to grasp! The wonder of why the church was not fulfilling John 14:12 often comes to mind: "He that believeth on me, the works that I do shall he do also; and greater works than these shall he do; because I go unto my Father." The realization is the church could not fulfill John 14:12 (KJV) until it first accepted in 1 John 4:17! Is it possible, we fail to operate in kingdom authority because we neglect our spiritual heritage (or who we are)?

Be Perfect

At the beginning of this book, I wrote briefly concerning perfection. One of the greatest fallacies in the church is the misunderstanding of the state of perfection. At the close of Jesus's Sermon on the Mount, he made a statement that has been, for the most part, greatly misunderstood. "Be ye therefore perfect, even as your Father which is in heaven is perfect" (Matthew 5:48 KJV). One definition of the word *perfect* is "complete" (Strong's Hebrew/Greek G5046). Many in the church today have spent their lifetime as Christians trying to perfect something that is already perfect or complete something that's already complete. If we are to be perfect and complete as our Father, which is in heaven, then we must have the same nature as our Father—which is in heaven. You can accomplish this by being born again. It is not something achieved; it is something that you receive!

The new world that you are now of has no imperfections. It is impossible for anyone to be born out of His world with spiritual birth defects. James 1:17 (KJV) declares this: "Every good gift and every perfect gift is from above, and cometh down from the Father of lights, with whom is no variableness, neither shadow of turning." The psalmist David declared in Psalms 139:14 (KJV), "I will praise thee; for I am fearfully and wonderfully made: marvelous are thy works; and that my soul knoweth right well." See, His works are marvelous and our soul needs to know this diligently!

When God our Creator sees us the way He created us, should we not see ourselves the same way? After Paul stated in 2 Corinthians 5:17 that we are new creations in Christ, he finished this thought by proclaiming these words: "For he hath made him to be sin for us, who knew no sin; that we might be made the righteousness of God in him" (2 Corinthians 5:21 KJV). When God, who created us through the new birth, sees us as His righteousness, should we not see ourselves as the same? We become irreverent when we see ourselves in any other way than how He sees us.

Righteousness is not something that we achieve. It is something that we receive through our new creation: Ephesians 4:24 (KJV), "And that ye put on the new man, which after God is created in righteousness and true holiness." It comes with the gift of the new birth! You don't get born again and then strive for these attributes; you were born again with these attributes! You were born again, perfect, righteous, and you were born again holy. "It is not of yourselves, it is the gift of God, Not of works, lest any man should boast" (Ephesians 2:8–9 KJV).

You Are the Branch

Let me explain it another way. Jesus in John 15:5 (KJV) alludes to Himself as the vine and the church as being the branch, "I am the vine, ye are the branches: He that abideth in me, and I in him, the same bringeth forth much fruit: for without me ye can do nothing. Jesus is the true vine, but notice what He says about the church…ye are the branches." He didn't say to *try* to be the branch. He said YOU ARE the branch!

The vine makes the branch what it is, not the branch itself. Without the vine, the branch ceases to be. However, with the vine, the branch can fulfill its intended purpose, which is to glorify the Father, "Herein is my Father glorified, that ye bear much fruit… What flows through the vine also flows through the branch making the branch inwardly the same as the vine" (John 15:8 KJV). Paul said it this way in Roman 11:16 (KJV), "If the root is holy, so are the branches."

The manifestation of fruit is contingent upon our connection to the vine. The sole responsibility of the branch is to bear fruit produced through connection to the vine. It all comes from within through connection! Bearing fruit should be as natural as inhaling and exhaling.

We never think about inhaling and exhaling; it is a natural act. So is bearing fruit a natural act. When I speak of fruit; I am talking about that which is manifested through the church because of our connection. The fruit is defined simply as the manifestation of the kingdom of God through the body of Christ.

This passage of scripture has been grossly misinterpreted and misrepresented by many teachers today and needs further explanation.

In John 15:2 (KJV), Jesus states, "Every branch in me that beareth not fruit he taketh away: and every branch that beareth fruit he purgeth it, that it may bring forth more fruit." Many teach if we are not bearing fruit to God's satisfaction; then He will kill us and take us on to heaven. Furthermore, if we are bearing fruit, then He will allow a calamity in our lives to purge us so we can bear more fruit. Who would want to serve a God of this magnitude? In the wildest of dreams, the comprehension of our loving Heavenly Father doing this to His children is absurd!

Through research and the study of the history of Israel and Palestine, I learned how the people of these areas worked their vineyards. This brought clarity to what Jesus was saying and not saying. When a young branch would begin to blossom but bore no fruit, the vinedresser would take the branch and lift it up from its position to a place where it's potential for bearing fruit could flourish. The words *taketh away* in verse 2 means to "lift up"! Jesus meant that if we were not bearing fruit, then He would lift us up (i.e., edify, encourage, build) so we could bear fruit. The purging process He was referring to is explained in verse 3: "Now ye are clean through the word which I have spoken to you."

The word *purgeth* in verse 2 comes from the same Greek word for "clean" (Strong's Greek/Hebrew G2513). The Word of God is what purges us—not calamity, nor destruction, nor sickness, or disease.

Fruit of the Womb

> Lo, children are a heritage of the LORD: and the fruit of the womb is his reward. (Psalms 127:3 KJV)

This passage has a literal and spiritual significance. Paul declares that all of us are children of God by faith in Jesus Christ (Galatians 3:26 KJV). In this respect, we are the fruit of God's womb because we were born out of God. You receive this gift by receiving Jesus Christ.

In natural birth, a child that is conceived within the womb of its mother, a wonderful thing takes place. It develops and grows inside the womb by receiving nourishment through the umbilical cord attached from the placenta of the mother to the fetus.

Psalms 62:5 (KJV) is an interesting passage of scripture concerning conceiving: "My soul, wait thou only upon God; for my expectation is from him." *Expectation*, also meaning "cord," is used for attachment (Strong's Hebrew/Greek H8615). The word *wait* in this passage translates as the word *rest* (Strong's Hebrew/Greek H1826). David was implying that his rest was complete in God only because he connected divinely to Him.

Just as the fetus receives nourishment and strength for maturation from its connection to the placenta of the mother, the church receives nourishment and strength for maturation from our connection to the Father by his Spirit. Now, do you see the achievement of perfection and completeness? It is only by a divine connection to God through Jesus Christ our Lord by His Spirit!

Another interesting note concerning the fetus is once it reaches maturity in the womb of its mother, it begins to break forth as fruit (be birthed) from the world it is of (the mother's womb) and into another world. Now that it is of a different world it no longer receives its nourishments the way it did from the old world. The fetus receives new nourishment in a new way. The same analogy applies to our spirit man. We are born again, not of the old fallen, sinful world but of heaven itself, the dwelling place of God—the very place of perfection and completeness! Paul stated this unto the church at Colossae,

> Giving thanks unto the Father, which hath made us meet to be partakers of the inheritance of the saints in light: Who hath delivered us from the power of darkness, [The old world] and hath translated us into the kingdom of his dear Son (the New World). (Colossians 1:12–13 KJV)

Now that our spirit's origin is of the new world, we must raise our soul to the level of our spirit.

CHAPTER 8

Seek Those Things Which Are Above

> If ye then be risen with Christ, seek those things which are above, where Christ sitteth on the right hand of God. Set your affection on things above, not on things on the earth. For ye are dead, and your life is hid with Christ in God. (Colossians 3:1–3 KJV)

Paul was making a valid point to the church at Colossae. Today, many have seemed to miss that point. To be *risen with Christ*, in verse 1, means to be born again. By Paul saying, *ye are dead* in verse 3, is an indication that you are no longer of the old world. "Your life is hidden with Christ in God" shows as of right now; you are of the same world that God is of through Jesus Christ, our Lord! The point Paul was making was to encourage the church to raise their souls to the level of their spirit. This is not God's responsibility; it is ours. Now that we are born again; our spirit is already in the place of *above,* which Paul mentions in verse 1. He explained with more detail in his letter to the Ephesians:

> Blessed be the God and Father of our Lord Jesus Christ, who hath blessed us with all spiritual blessings in heavenly places in Christ: Even when we were dead in sins, hath quickened us together with Christ, [by grace ye are saved]; And hath raised us up together, and made us sit together in heavenly places in Christ Jesus. (Ephesians 1:3; 2:5–6 KJV)

Did you hear what Paul was saying? He stated Christ "hath blessed[past tense meaning it is already done] us" with all spiritual blessings in heavenly places *right now* and being made alive with Christ we are now sitting with him in the heavenly places where the blessings are. It is a DONE DEAL! The church spends much of its time trying to get from God what he orchestrated within the inside of us.

Now that our spirit is in the place of *above*, Paul said in Colossians 3:2, we are now to set our affection on things above (raise our soul to the level of our spirit). The word *affection* means to exercise the mind (Strong's Greek/Hebrew G5426). Since one of the main components of our soul is our mind, Paul is saying we are to raise our soul (our mind and our thoughts) to the place of *above* or as Paul called it the heavenly place where our spirit already dwells with Christ. For the blessings to come forth into manifestation the way God intends, our thinking has to align with our spirit. The Spirit of God bears witness to the spirit of man, not his soul, that we are God's children, "The Spirit itself beareth witness with our spirit, that we are the children of God" (Romans 8:16 KJV).

Fruit Preserves

> And the very God of peace sanctify you wholly, and I pray God your whole spirit and soul and body be preserved blameless unto the coming of our Lord Jesus Christ.
> Faithful is he that calleth you, who also will do it. (1 Thessalonians 5:23–24)

As a young boy, I was privileged to be raised on a farm in rural Alabama, along with my older brother and two sisters, one being my twin. There, we raised our vegetables and fruits. It was a farm in every sense of the word. We also had cows, horses, pigs, and chickens. Dogs and cats were plentiful as well. My grandma made some of the best jellies, jams, and preserves I had ever eaten in my life; my favorite was blackberry. The wonderful delights made were from the fruit we harvested from our trees, vines, and bushes.

This is being shared with you in hopes of giving you a better understanding of what Paul meant in 1 Thessalonians 5:23–24. Often when I would read verse 23, I would think of grandma's preserves and of the time I would go with her to pick blackberries—with the job of looking for snakes lurking nearby. She would gather the fruit, and with the proper ingredients, she would concoct wonderful fruit preserves that would last indefinitely. Paul said that his prayer was that our whole spirit, soul, and body be *preserved* blameless. Our spirit, soul, and body are all the fruit of God. It is of the utmost importance we see our whole self—that way. God loves mankind, and what is important to him should be important to us. God does not want only the spirit of man preserved; he wants the soul and body preserved as well. Notice in verse 23 that Paul uses the word *whole* in reference to the whole spirit. The word *whole* is the Greek word *hol-ok'-lay-ros*, which means "complete to the end, absolutely perfect" (*Strong's Greek/Hebrew G3650* and *G2819*). What Paul means is that our spirit is wholly and totally complete and absolutely perfect simply because it has all the fullness of God for it is just like God. Is our soul and body complete and absolutely perfect? The answer is no. Will our physical body last forever? No, but like grandma's fruit preserves, it will last for an indefinite time. Will our spirit and soul last forever? Absolutely! Paul said it this way: "But though our outward man perish *[gradually decaying and getting older]*, yet the inward man is renewed *[fresh each and every day]* day by day" (2 Corinthians 4:16 KJV). Our spirit is fresh and new every day, twenty-four hours a day seven days a week. Our soul is designed to feed from our spirit preserving it throughout all eternity.

The word *preserve* in 1 Thessalonians 5:23 means "to guard against loss or injury by keeping the eye upon" (Strong's Hebrew/Greek G5083). *Webster* defines *preserve* to mean "to keep from harm or damage, to protect and save, to prepare for future use." Paul was praying for exactly this. He was praying the whole of man, spirit, soul, and body, which are the fruit of God, be saved, protected, kept from harm or injury, and prepared for use in God's kingdom on earth. In verse 24, Paul stated God is the faithful one that will do this through us by Jesus Christ! He is the one that preserves the whole fruit.

CHAPTER 9

The Order of Man

> And the Lord God formed man of the dust of the ground, (body) and breathed into his nostrils the breath of life; (spirit) and man became a living soul (soul). (Genesis 2:7 KJV)

We must understand the order of man created by God. First, there was the Spirit of God, or as verse 7 says, "the breath of life." The breath of life has always been and will always be the breath of life. It is God's Spirit, which was to have preeminence in the earth then and preeminence in the earth today. God has never backed away from that mandate! Second, God formed the body from the dust of the ground. He made an earthen vessel to house His Spirit on earth. Then God breathed His Spirit into man's nostrils so the man could become a living soul, not just a soul but a living soul (i.e., a breathing creature. Strong's Hebrew/Greek H5315). The man became a living soul because God's spirit fed through our spirit—the breath of life! The same is true today. The Spirit of God (breath of life) must feed man's soul to reach the level of maturation that Father intended.

JERRY ROBINSON

The Order of Man Tarnished

When Adam and Eve sinned, the whole of man was forfeited. The man became chaotic within himself, distorting the order God Himself established. No longer was the order of man spirit, soul, and body. Now the order was body, soul, and spirit because now the spirit of man was dead to God and could not dominate the whole of man as God intended from the beginning because the connection was now lost. Since the connection between our spirit and God's Spirit was broken, man lost the ability of God's spirit to lead him. The body (flesh) became the domineering force from which man's soul (i.e., his thinking, his desires, and his purposes) fed. Although man's spirit was still alive, it was separated from God and under complete control of the body and soul.

The serpent contended that if he could deceive man into trusting his soul for guidance rather than the spirit of God within, then it would cause the destruction of God's greatest creation. Because of this, man began to lead by his own animal appetites rather than God. He digressed rather than progressed. His soul was constantly toward evil to the point that it grieved God:

> And God saw that the wickedness of man was great in the earth, and that every imagination of the thoughts of his heart was only evil continually. And it repented the Lord that he had made man on the earth, and it grieved him at his heart. (Genesis 6:5–6 KJV)

Inspiration of God

God made good on the promise he gave to the serpent in Genesis 3:15, "And I will put enmity between thee and the woman, and between thy seed and her seed; it shall bruise thy head, and thou shalt bruise his heel." The word *seed* not only was referring prophetically to Jesus Christ; it also was referring to the church! *Seed* in this particular verse means "posterity" (Strong's Hebrew/Greek H2233), which means all future generations. God was informing the serpent (Satan) that He would restore order in His time, and the spirit of man would once again take precedence over the body and soul.

Paul wrote in 2 Timothy 3:16–17 (KJV):

> All scripture is given by inspiration of God, and is profitable for doctrine, for reproof, for correction, for instruction in righteousness: That the man of God may be perfect, thoroughly furnished unto all good works.

Inspiration in this passage means "divinely breathed in" (Strong's Hebrew/Greek G2315). Through the new birth, the Word Himself *is divinely breathed in* into one's person, reviving His Spirit, thereby reversing the chaotic order caused by the first Adam, fulfilling 1 Corinthians 15:22 (KJV), "For as in Adam all die, even so in Christ shall all be made alive."

The posterity of God is Jesus Christ and all of His brothers and sisters the church. Romans 8:17 (KJV) reads, "And if children, then heirs; heirs of God, and joint-heirs with Christ."

The seed of the serpent (lost humanity) fulfilled the bruising of the heel of the seed of the woman (Jesus Christ) at the cross. When Jesus cried in John 19:30 (KJV) that "it is finished," it brought about the climactic defeat of satanic authority over all that would receive Jesus as Savior and Lord! Now it is the responsibility of the posterity of God, which resurrected spiritually, to demonstrate the serpent's defeat by living victoriously in Christ.

Referring back to something of importance in chapter 3, I explained of Satan's demise and how that he was totally destroyed by the death of our Lord at the cross. I shared the Greek word for *destroyed* is the word *kat-arg-eh-o*, which means "to loosen and render entirely useless, void, and of none effect" (Strong's Hebrew/Greek2673). As a Christian, you no longer have a sin nature but a divine nature, for the sin nature has been destroyed. God replaced the old sinful nature with his divine non-sinful nature. We must understand and consider that even though the sinful nature is gone from our spirit, the remnant of that nature is still lurking in our minds.

The sinful nature was abolished instantaneously by being born again, but the effects of that nature still linger until *we* do something about it. I knew someone once who was bitten by a snake. He promptly killed the snake, but the damage already occurred. The poison was already in his body. Destroying the snake stopped him from ever biting anyone again, but the poison continued to work its way through his bloodstream. His system needed something administered into it before the poison would subside. Before the serpent was destroyed by Jesus' death at the cross, he poisoned humankind. However, just as the man that was bitten by the snake had to have something administered into his system to take care of the poison, Jesus empowered his church with something to take care of the poison that remained after his destruction. That *something* is Jesus Himself.

CHAPTER 10

Greater Is He That Is in You

> Ye are of God, little children, and have overcome them: because greater is he that is in you, than he that is in the world. (1 John 4:4 KJV)

When I first came across this passage of scripture, I began to look deep within myself for this "greater *in me*" it was referring to. I was taught, as a young Christian, that I had to live daily in a constant state of repentance, and even though I was born again, I was still looked upon by God as a sinner. The only difference was that now I was saved by grace. I suppose this is where the term *a sinner saved by grace* originated from, although I have yet to find that passage anywhere in the New Covenant scriptures.

As a Christian being taught *the constant state of repentance*, I was taught that I sinned every day, and all I had to do was repent by telling God I was sorry for the sin I committed on a daily basis. I was also taught that I had to ask God every day to forgive me of all my sin. What confused me the most was the fact that John said that the greater one was inside of me, yet most of the Christians that I had contact with acted like he that was in the world was greater than *He* that was in them! When I began to understand the word *repentance*, I began to understand the passage. The word *repent* means to think differently or reconsider (Strong's Hebrew/Greek G3340).

I realized John was teaching us to focus our thinking, to shift from he that is in the world (man) to He that is in us (Jesus)!

The Bible says in 1 John 3:8 (KJV), "He that committeth sin is of the devil; for the devil sinneth from the beginning." For this purpose, the Son of God was manifested, that He might destroy the works of the devil.

Jesus destroyed the devil, according to Hebrews 2:14. He has empowered the church to destroy his works. The word *destroy* in 1 John 3:8 is a different Greek word than destroy in Heb. 2:14. The Greek word for destroy in 1 John 3:8 is the word *Luo*, which means to put off what has been loosened and rendered entirely useless, void, and of none effect. Jesus destroyed the sin nature, and replaced it with a divine nature. He empowers the church to put off the residue or remnant of the sin nature by renewing our mind to the word.

A Constant State of Repentance

A constant state of repentance is acceptable if interpreted the right way in accordance to scripture. What does it mean to be in a constant state of repentance? In Matthew 4:17 (KJV), the Bible says, "From that time Jesus began to preach, and to say, Repent: for the kingdom of heaven is at hand." We must understand Jesus was addressing people schooled in the law. Therefore their thinking was in contrast to what Jesus was about to present to them. They thought that the kingdom of heaven would usher in by keeping the law. Many in the church today still have this same mindset, but Jesus came with a new doctrine he called the gospel. He stated the kingdom of heaven would become visible to those that would repent or change their way of thinking. Mark recorded the words of Jesus this way: "The time is fulfilled, and the kingdom of God is at hand: repent ye, and believe the gospel" (Mark 1:15 KJV).

Jesus was saying the time had come to where the kingdom of God would be manifested from within, and the principle of faith would bring about this manifestation:

> But before faith came, we were kept under the law, shut up unto the faith which should afterwards be revealed. Wherefore the law was our schoolmaster to bring us unto Christ, that we might be justified by faith. But after that faith is come, we are no longer under a schoolmaster. (Galatians 3:23–25 KJV)

Faith has arrived, and we are no longer under a schoolmaster (law)! Now that is the gospel!

Meaning of the Word *Gospel*

In the preface, I shared a few things concerning the Gospel. Now I want to go a little more in detail concerning its meaning.

The word *gospel* literally means "good news" (Strong's Hebrew/Greek G2098). The Greek word *Evangelion* means the *good message*. We will explore the Greek word *Evangelion* later in this section.

Paul wrote in his letter to the Romans in chapter 1, verse 16 (KJV), "For I am not ashamed of the gospel of Christ: for it is the power of God unto salvation to everyone that believeth."

Remember that we learned in chapter three that the word power is the Greek word *dunamis*, which means the inherent ability residing in a thing by virtue of its nature. Simply put, *dunamis* means *God-given ability*. When born again you were given the nature of God. God's ability always accompanies His nature; therefore, you also received the ability of God or *dunamis*. Note that Paul stated that the gospel of Christ is the power of God. I have asked scores of people over the years what the meaning of the word gospel meant, and for the most part none of them knew. Most of the ones I ask were either presently in church or were raised in church, and they didn't know what *gospel* meant. That's disturbing!

The gospel sums up as meaning, Jesus took our place upon the cross of sin so we could take His place eternally as sons of God! THAT'S GOOD NEWS! God took our place so we could take His! Is that not gospel? Is that not good news? This is what the angel of the Lord came to tell the shepherds who were abiding in a field keeping watch over their sheep. This is nothing more than allegories that serve as an example to shepherds (pastors) everywhere today who God calls to keep watch over their sheep:

> And there were in the same country shepherds abiding in the field, keeping watch over their flock by night. And, lo, the angel of the Lord came upon them, and the glory of the Lord shone round about them: and they were sore afraid. And the angel said unto them, Fear not: for, behold, I bring you good tidings of great joy, which shall be to all people. For unto you is born this day in the city of David a Saviour, which is Christ the Lord. (Luke 2:8–11 KJV)

THE GOSPEL REALLY IS GOOD NEWS

> The words "good tidings" are the same words for the word gospel.

The angel of the Lord was announcing the Gospel that's revealed through the Savior who is Christ the Lord. Listen very closely to the following verses: "And suddenly there was with the angel a multitude of the heavenly host praising God and saying; Glory to God in the highest, and on earth peace, good will toward men" (Luke 2:13–14 KJV).

First, notice that a multitude of the heavenly host was praising God and *saying* not praising God and singing as some might think. The word *saying* is the Greek word *lego*, which means "to give out, to point out, and to affirm" (Strong's Greek/Hebrew G3004). The heavenly host was giving out an affirmation or a prophetic word to the people. The prophetic word given was found in verse 14. The heavenly host was prophetically saying that the God of all glory in the heavens has come to earth to *reside in* man (the word *toward* literally means "in"), thereby establishing peace, purpose, and rest!

Today man may have changed the message. In truth, the message did not change! God has made peace with man!

> But watch thou in all things, endure afflictions, do the work of an evangelist, make full proof of thy ministry. (2 Timothy 4:5 KJV)

I previously shared with you that the word *Evangelion* means the "good message." *Evangelion* is from where we get the word evangelist. In the previous verse, Paul is instructing Timothy to do the work of an evangelist. So what is the work of an evangelist? The work of an evangelist is to announce the good message! Believe it or not, Paul never instructed anyone to preach hell or sin. On the contrary, he instructed everyone to preach Jesus! He instructed us to confess Jesus, not hell and not sin! Now that's good news!

> That if thou shalt confess with thy mouth the Lord Jesus, and shalt believe in thine heart that God hath raised him from the dead, thou shalt be saved.
> For with the heart man believeth unto righteousness; and with the mouth confession is made unto salvation. (Romans 10:9–10 KJV)

We get bombarded today with all kinds of beliefs concerning confession. The good news is that we do not have to spend the rest of our days confessing sin to our heavenly Father. If that were the case, we would have to keep up with every sin we have ever committed and confess all.

But Paul said, let's just confess Jesus and believe that confessing his name and not sin is what makes us righteous. Now that's good news! Now that's the gospel.

CHAPTER 11

Who Is His Son?

> Giving thanks unto the Father, which hath made us meet to be partakers of the inheritance of the saints in light. Who hath delivered us from the power of darkness, and hath translated us into the kingdom of his dear son. (Colossians 1:12–13 KJV)

As I stated in an earlier chapter, I have three other siblings, one being an older brother named Warren. Samuel Robinson was my late father. If someone were to walk into a crowded room, in which I was present and ask the question, "Who is the son of Samuel Robinson?" without hesitation, I would quickly reply, "I am!" If asked the question, "Who is the elder son of Samuel Robinson?" The reply would be Warren.

Today if you ask most Christians the question: Who is the son of God? without hesitation, their reply would be Jesus. In truth, Jesus is the elder son but not the ONLY son of God! Our thinking must shift to see ourselves as God sees us. We must see ourselves as SONS OF GOD!

JERRY ROBINSON

Only Begotten Son

> For God so loved the world, that He gave His only begotten son, that whosoever believeth in Him should not perish, but have everlasting life. (John 3:16 KJV)

The fulfillment of this passage took place because Jesus is NOT the *only begotten* son anymore! The words *only begotten* mean, *only born* (Greek/Hebrew G3439).

In John 1:14, John refers to Jesus as the only begotten son being full of grace and truth. Another fulfilled passage is John 1:14 (KJV), "And the Word was made flesh, and dwelt among us, (and we beheld his glory, the glory as of the only begotten of the Father,) full of grace and truth." Again we must see and understand that through the death, burial, and resurrection of our Lord and our acceptance of this truth, then we must conclude that Jesus isn't the only begotten of the Father any longer! He wants us to know this!

Another passage that alludes to the fact that Jesus is not the only begotten son of God is found in James 1:18 (KJV), "Of His own will begat he us with the word of truth, that we should be a kind of first fruits of his creatures." The word *begat* means to breed forth, to generate (Greek/Hebrew G616). It implies *birth*. See, it is his will to birth more sons. Paul again writes in Hebrews 2:10, "For it became him, for whom are all things, and by whom are all things, in bringing many *sons* unto glory, to make the captain of their salvation perfect through suffering." Did you notice what God's purpose is? To bring many SONS to glory. His purpose is to make more sons! He suffered to fulfill this. If we do not accept our son-ship, then His sufferings were in vain!

We are irreverent to God when we fail to accept and acknowledge who we now are in Christ and how God sees us!

I Don't Deserve It

One of the most erroneous statements which I hear constantly from believers is, "I don't deserve God's grace." Seeing ourselves from the standpoint of a sinner, I can very well understand this statement, but seeing ourselves from the standpoint of a saint makes this statement unequivocally wrong! As a son of God, we deserve every good thing that God has for us! You deserve it not because you have been good or bad. You deserve it simply because you are the son of God. You are an heir!

Chad, my son, from the very moment he could talk, has never come to me and said, "Dad, it's not fair that you give me this new toy because I don't deserve one." Or, "Dad, it's not fair that you give me these new clothes because I don't deserve them." Or, "Dad, it's not fair that you give me this car because I don't deserve it"—etc., etc. The deserving is not about fair-ship; it's about heir-ship!

> The spirit itself beareth witness with our spirit that we are the children (sons) of God And if children, (sons) then heirs; heirs of God, and joint-heirs with Christ. (Romans 8:16–17 KJV)

Notice that Paul said that as children of God, we are heirs of God! Did you also notice that he said we are joint-heirs with Christ? In God's eyes, we are just as much a son of God as Jesus is. The Spirit bears witness to this fact. We are irreverent to God if we do not bear witness to this!

I approached my son Chad once and said, "Son, what would you say if I told you that I was going to give all that I own and all that I possess to someone else rather than to you." He replies, "Dad, that wouldn't be right! I am your sole heir. It rightfully belongs to me because I am your son. I deserve it!" God wants His children to approach Him in the same way, with boldness in knowing and confessing who we are.

> Seeing then that we have a great high priest that is passed into the heavens, Jesus the Son of God; let us hold fast our profession (confession). For we have not an high priest which cannot be touched with the feeling of our infirmities; but was in all points tempted like as we are, yet without sin. Let us therefore come boldly unto the throne of grace that we may obtain mercy, and find grace to help in time of need. (Hebrews 4:14–16 KJV)

Today as joint-heirs with Jesus Christ, we have every right to boldly claim, not with arrogance but with confidence, our inheritance. We have the right to go before the throne of grace to ask for help, not because we earned it, but because it was gifted to us through Jesus Christ our Lord.

Conclusion

> Study to shew thyself approved unto God, a workman that needeth not to be ashamed, rightly dividing the word of truth. (2 Timothy 2:15 KJV)

As a student of the Bible, I can attest to the fact that I have spent countless hours in Bible study. My goal was to learn as much scripture as possible for a couple of reasons. One reason was so I would have a reservoir of scriptural knowledge so I could recall a passage from memory if needed at any given time. But the main reason for my extensive study was so God would approve of me.

My thinking was that the more scripture I knew, the more God would approve of me. It wasn't until years later that I began to understand what Paul was and wasn't saying to Timothy in this passage. He wasn't telling Timothy to study hard so God would put His stamp of approval on him. Paul was telling Timothy that God had already accepted him in Christ! *Study* in the Greek is the word *spoudazō* (Greek/Hebrew G4707). It means to make every effort, to labor. This same Greek word is used in Hebrews 4:11 (KJV), "Let us labour (or study) therefore to enter into that rest, lest any man fall after the same example of unbelief."

The writer of Hebrews was saying that our responsibility is to make every effort or labor to enter into rest, not work!

In other words, our labor is to rest, and the rest is that God approves of YOU! Paul was telling Timothy in 2 Timothy 2:15 to study or make every effort or labor to show *thyself* that God accepts you! You must show (prove) to YOURSELF who you really are in Christ Jesus! James wrote in the book of James chapter 2, verse 20 (KJV): "But wilt thou know, O vain man, that faith without works is dead?"

This passage is most often taught that if we aren't working by observing all the ordinances then our faith is dead. That definition simply isn't true! This passage literally means that faith without Jesus' finished work at the cross and resurrection from the grave is dead. Look how Paul explained this in 1 Corinthians 15:14 (KJV), "And if Christ be not risen, then is our preaching vain, and your faith is also vain."

Understand that it's Jesus's works not our works that moves Father to bless us. Our work is only to believe. John 6:29 (KJV), "Jesus answered and said unto them, This is the work of God, that ye believe on him whom he hath sent."

That is the Gospel! That is good news!

Helpful

Second Corinthians 13:1 states, "In the mouth of two or three witnesses shall every word be established."

Paul said in the above passage that two or three witnesses are all it takes to establish a truth. Yet throughout this book, I have compiled approximately 150 passages of scripture that give witness to the gospel of Jesus Christ.

My hope is that this book has been insightful in helping you understand what resonates within you, the believer. My desire after reading this book is that you will take a second look at the cross and hopefully gain a greater understanding of what really happened that day at Calvary and how God finished in Jesus what He began in Adam. What Adam wouldn't allow God to do through him, Jesus allowed God to do through Him, thereby creating a new species of people made in the exact image *(likeness)* of their Creator NOW! That's the Gospel. That's the Good News! The Gospel really is good news!

> *It is finished.*
> —John 19:30 (KJV)

Acknowledgments

This book has been fifteen years in the making. I say fifteen years because it was about that time that I began to make the transition from preaching a doctrine that was based solely on what we must do for eternal life to preaching the good news *(gospel)* of what Jesus has done to attain our eternal life. There were times I thought I would never finish it. However, through the love and support of friends and family, this book finally came to fruition. I want to acknowledge everyone who participated in this work; without which, it never would have been completed.

I wish to thank my friend Karie Raburn, who was the first to read the rough draft. She spent hours reading and rereading my book, correcting my spelling, grammar, punctuation, run-on sentences, etc. She helped to make this book presentable to my publisher.

To another friend, Wes Jones, in whom I give thanks, who was instrumental in helping me not only by encouraging me to get this book into the hands of the reader but also by finding the right publisher.

I want to give thanks to Michele Robertson, who, after reading this work, stated that the book was easy to read and understand and that it is relevant for the church today.

I give thanks to the coordinators, editors, and all the staff of Page Publishing Inc. who helped make this book a reality.

JERRY ROBINSON

Finally, I want to thank my wife, Shelia, for running interference for me through all the hours I spent in my study writing by answering phone calls, entertaining people, grandchildren, etc.